FOUNDING DIRECTOR'S PREFACE

FOR THE PAST 45 YEARS I have nurtured a passion for Inuit art, a passion that I kept mostly to myself and my friends. The Musée d'art INUIT Brousseau came into being so that I could share this passion with all of you, and safeguard this rare collection.

The phenomenon of how Inuit art developed through time and space is unique in the world and in the history of art. Isolated for thousands of years in vast northern expanses, confronted with an extreme climate, these hunter-artists produced works that speak of qualities indispensable to their daily survival: infinite patience, extraordinary powers of observation, and an unlimited imagination.

Inuit artistic expression encompasses every aspect of the life of the people, whether nomadic or sedentary. Men, women, children, animals, legends, spirits, and mythology all give rise to a great variety of original works. Inuit art evolves, as does every living art, by drawing on its cultural references in a constantly changing world, and moulding it into contemporary forms.

I have long dreamed of exhibiting these works of art in a museum so that people could better understand and appreciate them: my wish is to introduce you to an exceptional culture and group of artists. This booklet is an additional introduction to their fascinating world.

RAYMOND BROUSSEAU

Founding Director of the Musée d'art INUIT Bro

Europeans arrive in the North: explorers, missionaries, whalers.

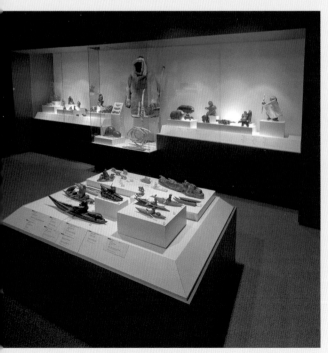

Various sculptures depicting the subject of *Inuit Women*

A hunter's world: travels by sled and kayak.
The animals Inuit life depended upon, and some rare artefacts.

INTRODUCTION

The Musée d'art INUIT Brousseau is first of all a tangible homage to the artists of the Canadian Arctic Circle, to their skills as sculptors and their technical ingenuity. These works represent the principal emissaries of an ancient people whose tradition has been passed down orally, works that play a crucial role in spreading Inuit culture throughout the world.

This art emerges from the distant past but also bears the future. It is a tribute to a traditional way of life, an inhospitable and even brutal environment, an incredible adaptability, the rich animal life in a hunter's world, and a symbolic and legendary universe peopled with superhuman beings and mythical animals.

This abundant and exotic world of the imagination is combined with a very contemporary realism reflecting the individual artist's sensibility. A personal vision of a world that is constantly changing translates into astonishing forms born of stone, bone, ivory or antler. This vision is a far cry from primitive folk art.

While containing some remarkable ethnographic and archaeological artefacts, the Musée d'art INUIT Brousseau is primarily a museum of art. To illustrate the context and evolution of Inuit aesthetic sensibility, works of the collective imagination that are more than 1000 years old are shown in conjunction with sculptures, drawings and engravings produced over the past 50 years.

The Musée d'art INUIT Brousseau

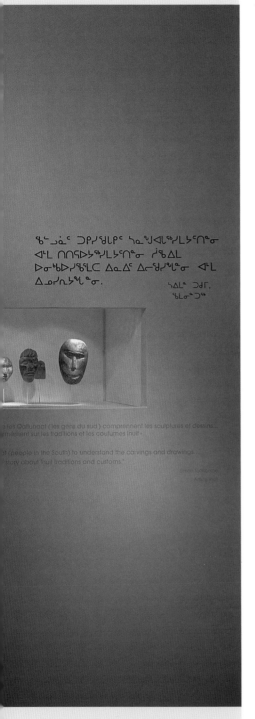

ˢᵇᶜᵔᴗᵃᶜ ᐅᑭᕆᔐᒪᑭᶜ ᓴᓇᵊᒍᐊᒡᔐᕐᒪᔐᶜᑌᵊᓂ ᐊᒡᒪ ᑎᑎᓯᐅᔐᵊᒍᔐᒪᔐᶜᑌᵊᓂᓂᓴ ᓍᵊᐃᒪ ᐅᓂᵊᑳᐅᒐᵊᐃᒪᑕ ᐃᓇᐃᶜ ᐃᓕᐅᒐᵊᕻᒐᓂ ᐊᒡᒪ ᐃᓗᕐᓇᒐᵊᕻᵃᓂ. ᓴᐃᒪᶜ ᐅᒡ� ᵊᑲᓗᓇᵊᑕᵃ

ANYONE WHO HAS KNOWN THE ARCTIC has also known that endless polar night that descends in stillness from the heavens, sometimes accompanied by those shimmering bolts of iridescence known as the aurora borealis. Waiting for the return of long days and the midnight sun, daily life thrives under this bluish half-light set with the stars that bound and envelop the land of the Inuit.

An intriguing row of faces and masks greets the visitor at the entrance. A foretaste of the exceptional warmth and magic of the North, they are in various forms and styles, carved in wood, whalebone and antler. The soothing blue surroundings evoke the immensity of the north and the boreal winter, suffusing the museum in a calm and intimate light that contrasts sharply with the busy tourist atmosphere of the Rue Saint-Louis.

Entrance showcase.
Visitors are greeted
by Inuit faces.

INUIT ART:
A SOUTHERN EXPOSURE

The Musée d'art INUIT Brousseau, founded in 1998, is the first museum south of the Arctic devoted exclusively to Inuit art and culture. It opened to the public on May 1, 1999.

The museum is the fruit of one person's abiding passion, and of the need to house and exhibit one of the finest private collections in Canada. The mission of the museum is to conserve, document and interpret past and future illustrations of this northern art whose eloquence and sculptural beauty have been recognized for over 50 years.

This museum would not exist were it not for the ever increasing public interest in this art form. The Musée d'art INUIT Brousseau chose a location in the heart of the busy historic district of Old Quebec so that a varied public, amateur and expert, local and overseas visitors, adults and school children, could all benefit from a permanent exhibition of this unique artistic heritage and many of its greatest masterpieces.

Qiatsuq Shaa, (1971-1997)
Cape Dorset
Dancing Bear, 1997
serpentinite
1998.424
28.6 × 22.2 × 12.7 cm

INTERNATIONAL SCOPE

The museum was first a private corporation, and since November 2000, a non-profit organization. It was enthusiastically welcomed into a select circle of international museums, adding legitimacy and urgency to its mandate and to the expansion of its overseas audience.

Strong links formed from the outset, leading to fruitful collaborations with eminent specialists (museologists, art historians, ethnologists, anthropologists, etc.) who confirmed the value of the museum's content and recognized the rigour of its presentations. It rapidly gained an international reputation, developing exclusive partnerships with some of the most prestigious museums in Europe and North America wishing to exhibit some of its pieces.

The museum building is a few steps from the Château Frontenac.

First acquisition 1958.

Artist unknown
Inukjuak
Igloo Spirit, circa 1950
steatite, ivory
1998.243
11 × 10 × 9 cm

Recent Acquisition
2002.

Artist unknown
Repulse Bay
Igloo Spirit,
circa 1950
Steatite
1998.027
15 × 4 × 9 cm
Photo Louise Leblanc

THE WORK OF A COLLECTOR

Raymond Brousseau's dream of a museum took shape slowly. He bought his first Inuit sculpture in 1958 while still a penniless student. Its formal individuality and expressive force had hooked or "harpooned" him for good: he continued collecting, continuously and meticulously, for the next 45 years, and gave up his career as a National Film Board director to open his first gallery.

With the opening of the first gallery, *Aux Multiples Collections,* in 1974, followed in 1986 and 1992 by two others, including *Galerie d'art Inuit Brousseau et Brousseau,* he established one of the most reputable Inuit art businesses in the country. Always in touch with what is currently being created in the North, Raymond Brousseau plays a seminal role in its dissemination. He has both improved the quality of the work and stimulated creativity by raising the standards for Inuit cooperatives that distribute to southern markets.

His judgement has been honed by expertise gained through extensive contact with artists' agents in Inuit villages, as well as by many years of personal observation regarding artists, styles, aesthetics and ethnography, so that for his own collection he keeps only the most significant works of any artist, region, technique or time period.

When the idea for this museum was born, in about 1985, he and his wife Lyse, a museographer, formed an ideal partnership for the design, planning, organizing and accomplishing of the project. With the purchase in 1995 of a large exhibition space on the ground floor of the Maisons Beaucourt, a new building close to the famous Château Frontenac in Old Quebec, their dream finally came true.

As the curator, Raymond Brousseau has added to the collection over the past 15 years with significant acquisitions that shed new light on the history of Inuit culture, art, and artists.

Caribou corner

Inuit mythology area:
legends and shamanism.

Another view of the temporary exhibition area.

THE EXHIBITION AREA

At the cutting edge of modern muse-
ology, the scenographic design by Lyse
Brousseau transports visitors out of the
everyday and into a voyage of discovery.
Using a sensitive arrangement of space,
four permanent exhibition rooms are
organized into sequential thematic groupings. Every new turn offers a learning
experience and a richly exotic perspective.

This educational journey consists of
more than 500 works of art interspersed
with maps, explanatory texts and video
extracts. After first contact with the Inuit
people, the evolution of their art, their
famous masters, the materials they use
and their sources of inspiration, the visit
concludes with a short film featuring the
artists at work.

Temporary exhibition area,
showing *Inuit Women, Women Artists*.

A separate area is reserved for temporary exhibitions that are renewed
annually. These enable visitors to explore
a particular aspect of Inuit art, and serve
as the basis for travelling thematic
exhibitions.

THE COLLECTION

The Musée d'art INUIT Brousseau collection is the result of one man's critical sense honed by four decades of judicious selection from amongst thousands of works of art. Ever expanding, the collection consists of more than 1000 works, particularly carvings, engravings, original drawings and, to a lesser extent, artefacts of exceptional historical and documentary interest such as statuettes, figurines, tools, clothes, hunting and fishing equipment, etc.

The museum is carefully designed to display every angle of the development of Inuit art, from its origins to the present day, pausing to focus on principal artists, specific styles, regional distinctions, the diversity of material and technique, artistic periods, and many other thematic groupings.

In large public institutions Inuit art is under-represented compared to other art, or else subsumed under the generic title of Native Art. The specialization of this museum has enabled it to acquire and make publicly accessible at all times the most complete panorama of contemporary Inuit art in Canada.

Shorty Killiktee, (1948-1993)
Kimmirut
Bear
serpentinite
2002.030
27.7 × 32.5 × 19.2 cm

Simon Hiqiniq, (born 1951)
Gjoa Haven
Giant Lifting a Woman, 1988
pyroxene, caribou antler
1998.447
67.3 × 47.5 × 30.7 cm

John Kavik, (1897-1993)
Rankin Inlet
Bust, circa 1970
basalt
1998.580
25 × 16.5 × 9.3 cm

Pauta Saila, (born 1916)
Cape Dorset
Bear, circa 1950
steatite, ivory
1998.459
21.2 × 8.5 × 9.1 cm

Kiakshuk, (1886-1966)
Cape Dorset
Standing Woman, circa 1955
serpentinite
1998.169
2.3 × 1.2 × 9 cm

Joe Talirunili, (1906-1976)
Puvirnituq
Kneeling Inuk, circa 1950
steatite
1999.031
9 × 13.5 × 7 cm

Artist unknown
Keewatin District
Woman's face with tattoos,
circa 20th century
basalt
14 × 10.5 × 2.5 cm

II

A thousand year old culture

Artist unknown
Clyde River
Face, circa 1950
whalebone
2002.091
20.3 × 15 × 7.5 cm

INUIT became accustomed to Canadian extremes four thousand years ago, and use many descriptive terms to name their white reality, snow (*aniu*, *apiiqqun*, *apak*, *mahak*, etc.) As they moved from their summering to their wintering grounds, from west to east, all the way to Greenland, their ancestors took possession of a land of cold and wind as vast as a continent. The Cree, their Indian neighbours, named them "Eskimos" or "eaters of raw meat". But on this land of Cain that they inhabit, they alone have been able to extract its riches, appreciate its charms and avoid its dangers, and thus they deserve to be called Inuit[1], "the people".

A NORTHERN REALM

Of the 150,000 people of the world's Arctic population who live north of the 55th parallel, around 45,000 are Canadian Inuit. In about 50 villages of between 300 and 1300 inhabitants each, the Inuit occupy a vast area extending from the Alaska border to Labrador, including Nunavut and Nunavik (Northern Quebec). This area, three million square kilometres (or a million square miles), would cover most of Europe and is five times the size of France. It is at once breathtakingly immense in size and infinitesimal in population.

---

1. Current usage tends to drop the term *Inuk*,
    retaining *Inuit* as the noun as well as the adjective.

This wilderness domain petrified in permafrost, veined with endless shorelines, riven by deep fjords, sown with rocky mountains, worn into mossy plains and spotted with crystalline lakes all the way down south to the treeline where the Indians live, this is the land the Inuit rejoice in calling *nunatsiaq*, "the beautiful land." · from *The Beautiful Land* by Ingo Hessel.

THE LAST HABITABLE PLACE IN THE WORLD

The first humans in the Canadian Arctic followed the sea and land mammals by crossing the ice floes in successive waves from Siberia via the Bering Strait and Alaska. The prehistoric process of population began 4000 years ago with the Dorset and later, the Thule or Thulean cultures, ancestors of today's Inuit. It took firm root in the last "habitable" part of the world with a second great migration early in the first 1000 years CE.

Artist unknown
St. Lawrence Island, Alaska
Female figure, Thule culture
ivory
8.5 × 2 cm
(Torngat Mountains, Labrador
Photograph by Eugène Kedl.)

A SURVIVAL PEOPLE

In the tundra, that desert of stone and ice where a moment of distraction could spell danger or death, where a fragment of wood from a shipwreck represents untold treasure, the survival instinct has always inspired toughness and self-sufficiency. Nomad hunters throughout the ages adapted and evolved in spite of the scarcity or absence of what even the toughest southerners would consider bare necessities.

Tracking large game (whales, seal, walrus, caribou, muskox, polar bear), processing the hides to make warm clothing, pulling sleds, constructing shelters out of practically nothing to stave off periodic famine, intense cold and blinding blizzards, all required a mobilization of energy and a sharing of tasks among the members of a clan, among blood relatives, and between men and women.

As surviving alone against the pitiless elements was impossible, these relationships of mutual aid and interdependence bonded a society divided into small communities, often extended families with little in the way of hierarchy who met only for seasonal gatherings. All shared the fruit of essential collective activities under the auspices of the shaman, or *angatkuk*, a healer who possessed occult powers and mediated between human beings and the gods.

Age-old isolation and the fierce struggle against the elements resulted in a survival people whose way of life changed little for several millennia, but which began to change drastically over the past 50 years.

(Pierre) Nauya, (1914-1977)
Rankin Inlet
European Sailboat, circa 1965
steatite, skin, caribou antler,
ivory, braided sinew and copper
1998.088
39.2 × 29.3 × 7.5 cm

Ross Kayotak, (born 1969)
Igloolik
Whaling, 1998
pyroxene, caribou antler
1998.107
16 × 40 × 30 cm

ENCOUNTER WITH THE *QUALLUNAAT*

The era of Arctic exploration began in the 1500s with the first contact with Europeans, *quallunaat* or "the men with thick eyebrows." Over the next three centuries European explorers looking for the Northwest Passage, whalers, fur traders and then missionaries of every confession (Moravians, Anglicans and Catholics) brought new tools, more effective weapons, strange new foods and religious practices that signalled the end of their age-old animist and shamanist customs and beliefs.

The new arrivals were later joined by scientists: anthropologists, ethnologists, geologists and archaeologists. They survived in this hostile environment thanks to the unrivalled experience of the Inuit, with whom they established a barter system, learning hunting methods, taking down their stories and marvelling at their ingenious inventions: the igloo, the kayak, the parka, float-harpoons, dogsled harnesses, articulated sleds etc.

Joanassie Korgak
Iqaluit
Igloo Scene, 2001
serpentinite, ivory, metal
3.5 × 38.6 × 18.5 cm

Artist unknown
Greenland
Figure in Kayak, circa 1920
wood, skin, ivory, sinew
1998.043
1.25 × 6.7 × 9 cm

Artist unknown
Labrador
Sled voyage, circa 1960
ivory, skin
7 × 5 × 22 cm

A PERIOD OF TRANSITION AND UPHEAVAL

These exchanges were timid and sporadic at first, but intensified in the 1700s and especially in the 1800s with the establishment of trading posts and permanent missions on the Labrador Coast, on Baffin Island, and on the shores of Ungava and Hudson Bay. As inland penetration was slow, certain Inuit family groups scattered throughout the less accessible and uncharted interior remained cut off from the world and suffered devastating famines until the 1950s.

In spite of the material and spiritual upheavals provoked by the intrusion of European culture, not to mention the assault of new germs (tuberculosis, diphtheria, flu, etc.) that decimated an already fragile Inuit population, it is only very recently that their lifestyle, hitherto practically immutable, has been profoundly disturbed, even revolutionized.

THE END OF A WORLD

The presence of southerners, to which the Inuit have grown accustomed over the past two centuries, was solidified when Canada affirmed sovereignty over the Arctic between 1895 and 1911, and a little later took charge of administration and justice.

With the approach of World War II and then the Cold War, the irreversible trend towards sedentarization accelerated as Canada responded to US pressures to build a national pan-continental shield against the communist threat, and saw the need to provide its Arctic population with continuing assistance in health and education.

The establishment of villages around trading posts, missions and military bases hastened the erosion of traditional values and ultimately the abandonment of an ancestral way of life. From the 1960s on the Inuit made their spectacular but inevitable début in the modern world.

Artist unknown
Three Miniature Figures, Thule culture
ivory
A 24 mm × 5 mm × 2.5 mm - B 20 mm × 4 mm × 2.5 mm - C 27 mm × 9 mm × 2.5 mm

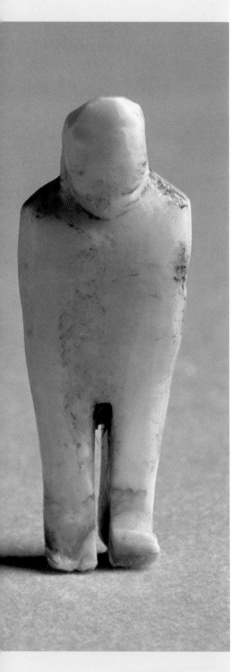

III

Discovering
Inuit art

THERE WAS A LONG SILENCE on the roof of the world. An eternity passed without a single echo from the outside world, without even a suspicion that another reality might exist, the southern reality with its *qallunaat* or *kabloona*, the non-Inuit. But then who from "down south" would have ever thought that one day a voice would rise out of that frozen and petrified land and, within a few decades, make known the Inuit? Art, or the concept of *sananguak*, meaning "crafted or carved copies of reality"[2] was that gift of universal language bestowed on the Inuit. They could finally tell their story to the world.

ART FROM THE FAR REACHES OF TIME

A cold, arid climate and meagre vegetation have enabled some rare and ancient sites of human occupation to be uniquely preserved. Modern archaeologists have made important discoveries even on the surface of the permafrost. Digs have unearthed small objects used for work or pleasure, carved or engraved in stone, ivory, bone or antler. These remains date from the Dorset and Thule cultures of a thousand years ago, and have their own distinct aesthetic and style.

---

2. There is no Inuktitut word for art, at least in the western sense of the word. Etymologically, the word *Sananguaq* comes from *sana*, meaning "to make" and *nguaq*, meaning "an imitation or replica of reality." George Swinton, *Sculpture of the Inuit*, p. 129-130.

These precious "relics" from the far reaches of time appear to be the earliest manifestations of Arctic art. They are portable for constant travel, and imbued with magic, while the use of natural forms in some and stylized designs in others are evidence of aesthetic concerns. Generations to come would draw their creative powers from this inexhaustible source.

Artist unknown
Seated Figure, circa 1900
ivory
4.8 × 2 × 3.5 cm

Artist unknown
Set of Eight Birds, Thule culture
ivory
various sizes (from 10 mm to 30 mm across)

Artist unknown
Drum Handle with Shaman Figure,
20th century
ivory
3 × 11.8 × 3.5 cm

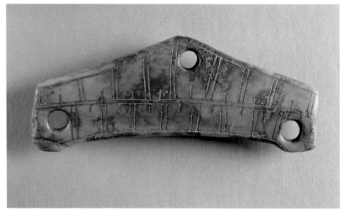

Artist unknown
St Lawrence Island, Alaska
Seal drag, Thule culture
incised ivory
3.5 × 10.5 × 0.5 cm

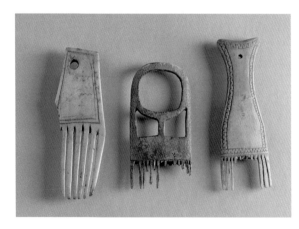

Artist unknown
Bering Strait
Three Combs, Thule culture
ivory
A   84 mm × 25 mm × 4 mm
B   60 mm × 35 mm × 3 mm
C   86 mm × 28 mm × 3 mm

A PRECIOUS TRADE COMMODITY

The arrival of outsiders had many implications, including the slow but sure death of a self-sufficient subsistence economy. The Inuit had no concept of trade, but quickly took to the barter system. Imported goods and provisions such as tobacco, tea, alcohol, coloured cloth, and especially guns and metal utility objects such as knives and other hunting and fishing equipment soon became practically indispensable.

The Inuit bartered furs, fancy clothing and local hunting and fishing products with the crews of explorers and whalers, and then with missionaries and resident traders. They also made souvenirs of uneven quality carved almost exclusively out of the walrus and narwhal ivory that was seen as most precious by passing outsiders, and solely to satisfy their tastes and curiosity.

"Nothing new was seen at this visit, if I except a most ingenious piece of carving from the grinder of a walrus; this was a very spirited little figure of a dog lying down and gnawing a bone; and although not much above an inch in length, the animal's general expression was admirable. I should, however, mention that we also procured a few little ivory bears of the same description, and far better executed than any we had purchased before." From the journal of Captain G. F. Lyon, Repulse Bay, September 25, 1824, cited by George Swinton in Sculpture of the Inuit, *p. 119.*

This trade commodity, current during the Historic Period (1771-1948), included human figures, toys and miniature camp scenes, igloos, and familiar animals. In spite of their "primitive nature", dictated by demand, many of the carvings are more than folk handicrafts. They reveal instead astonishingly careful execution, and are powerfully evocative works of art in their own right.

FROM TRADING ART TO MARKETING IT

Canadian government authorities saw artistic creation as a viable solution to Inuit economic problems and so, paradoxically, it was in the context of increasing Inuit dependence on southern society that artistic creation began to flourish 50 years ago. In the Contemporary Period (from 1948 until the present) the upset of sedentarization coincided with the beginning of national affirmation of Inuit art, followed by international recognition.

It was the Canadian Handicrafts Guild in Montreal that took the first interest. The exhibition of native arts that they organized in 1930 resulted in the many Inuit pieces on display being considered officially as works of art. This first attempt at commercialization, abandoned soon after with the advent of the Great Depression and World War II, only revived in 1948 due to the passionate enthusiasm of a young artist named James Houston. On his first trip to Inukjuak (Nunavik), he was astounded by the artistic potential of the artists of the Great North, to the point of devoting his entire career to promoting them throughout Canada and the United States.

Isapik Qanguq, (born 1918)
Pond Inlet
Walrus on Ice Floe
serpentinite, ivory
2002.084
11.7 × 17.8 × 13.6 cm

Isa Oomayoualook, (born 1915)
Inukjuak
Man Hunting Seal, circa 1950
steatite, sinew, antler
1998.028
18.8 × 15.8 × 9 cm

Several pieces dating from the early days
of commerce with South, 1950s-60s.

RECOGNITION

With Houston's initiatives art became a profitable local commercial industry for the Inuit. Inuit-owned cooperatives, established in the 1960s, protected the artists' interests, distributed their works in the south and preserved their authenticity.

With the World's Fair in Montreal in 1967, and the publication of an exhaustive and indispensable study by Professor George Swinton entitled *Art of the Inuit* (1971), the world finally trained its sights on this new art form.

Since then Inuit art has been constantly gaining in popularity, and is prized by international experts and collectors from every continent.

Paulosie Kasudluak, (born 1938)
Inukjuak
Hunter, circa 1960
steatite, ivory
1998.031
15 × 22.7 × 11.2 cm

Sponsored by the Guild of Montreal, the Hudson's Bay Company as the intermediary for purchase *in situ*, and the federal government as the principal backer, his involvement was a resounding success. A series of important exhibitions followed throughout the 1950s, including one at the National Gallery of Canada in Ottawa and another at Gimpel Fils in London.

Samson Nastapoka, (born 1931)
Inukjuak
Stone Carver, 1966
steatite
1998.039
22.5 × 34.5 × 10 cm

IV

Inuit art as timeless:
*technical and
stylistic aspects*

**FOR GENERATIONS INUIT have been hand-making clothes,
tools, hunting weapons and other articles of subsistence,
from the *qullik*, an oil lamp that also serves as a heater,
to the sharpest harpoon heads consecrated with incanta-
tory symbols. The time taken to create everything needed
to maintain a spark of light and heat in an igloo or tent,
to make possible the breath of life itself, has made of the
Inuit an shrewd artisan and a born sculptor.**

AN INHERITANCE OF SKILLS

Deeply rooted in their complementary
destinies, Inuit men and women passed
down the ancestral gestures of survival. The
honour of the man-hunter, who lay in wait
for game, depended on how effective were
the weapons and boats he himself had
designed and built with the scarce materials
available. His artistic skill lay above all in his
infinite patience and powers of observation,
fine-tuned by long periods waiting for prey.

Barnabus Arnasungaaq, (born 1924)
Baker Lake
Sculptor at Work, 1990
basalt
2002.023
24 × 21.5 × 18 cm

27

Jaco Ishulutaq, (born 1951)
Pangnirtung
Couple at Work, 1987
whalebone, caribou antler, skin
2002.030
36 × 92 × 40 cm

Using the same intrinsic qualities, the woman-mother and seamstress applied her talent and meticulous dexterity to every other aspect of traditional domestic life, and children, too, learned these skills by observing their parents.

Art, and particularly sculpture, is a domain in which women play as important a role as the men, and is learned through the same kind of apprenticeship. Art is thus perpetuated through observation, from father to son and from mother to daughter. Hence certain families today have several recognized artists among their members, giving rise to prominent dynasties that have made art their living heritage.

Elijah Kuppak, (1903-1979)
Arctic Bay
Figure with a Telescope, circa 1960
steatite
18.1 × 9.8 × 16 cm

Joanassie Smith, (1925-1963)
Puvirnituq
Spring Migration, circa 1960
serpentinite, sinew
2000.095
10.2 × 45.9 × 11.4 cm

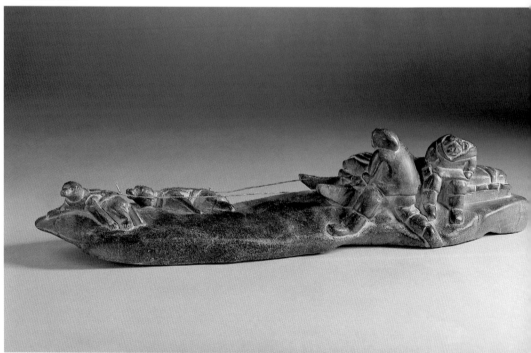

Pootoogook Jaw, (born 1959)
Cape Dorset
Fishing Scene, 1994
serpentinite, caribou antler, sinew, metal
1998.448
54 × 56.5 × 29.2 cm

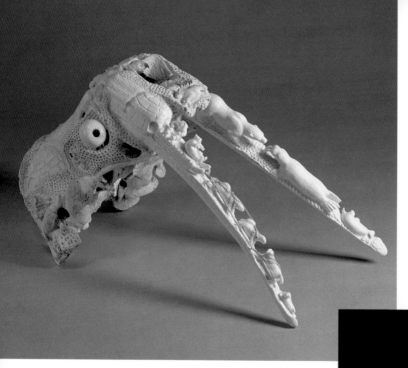

Luke Airut, (born 1942)
Igloolik
Carved Walrus Skull, 1990
bone, ivory, stone
2002.005
30 × 56 × 28 cm

THE ART OF RECYCLING

Long before the term became fashionable, recycling or re-using was integral to Inuit custom. In this sparse land where nothing could be lost or wasted, art made use of every scrap of inedible remains from the hunt and of lucky finds along shorelines or in the back country. Long before they used stone, artists used whalebone, antler, and especially ivory, which was both durable and beautiful.

FROM IVORY TO STONE

Walrus and narwhal ivory, once coveted by the Europeans, had become scarce by the mid-1900s. First generation Inuit artists turned to stone, a material that could be found in their vast rocky terrain.

Towkie Karpik, (born 1935)
Pangnirtung
Sculpted Narwhal Tusk, 1994
ivory
1.42 × 32 × 22 cm

Artist unknown
Inukjuak
Walrus, 1955
steatite
2002.083
12.5 × 18 × 26.3 cm

Aoudla Pee, (born 1920)
Cape Dorset
Bird, 1989
serpentinite
24 × 8.5 × 18.5 cm

Scattered through with veins of steatite (commonly known as soapstone), serpentinite, basalt, argillite, dolomite, quartz and even white marble, the tundra offers a diversity of local variety and colour, from greys to blues and greens, from pure white to jet black.

All the surrounding rock was not necessarily appropriate for carving, however. Sculptors looking for quality stone would travel long distances to look for a new seam. Methods of extraction were later improved, and cooperatives became the principal source of stone, organizing collective stone quarrying and sometimes even importing this precious basic material from the south.

ATTUNED TO THEIR MATERIAL

Self-taught Inuit artists work outside all established conventions, without preliminary sketches or preparation other than calling on their visual culture and their uncanny ability to possess and master the raw material, not changing or coercing it, but letting it reveal itself. The artist studies the original shape of the rock or whalebone from every angle and examines every protrusion, and this is what guides his or her hand, inspires the subject matter and determines the composition. This principle of the emergent form, or the "hidden subject" is one of the fundamental characteristics of the Inuit aesthetic.

Tools that belonged to sculptor George Arluk.

"There was no variety to the tools in the early days. I was able to buy only files and chipper, a chisel. But you could work ivory very well with this kind of tool. You would have to keep sharpening it. When you polished the ivory it came out very nicely. Yes, it was a big change to start working with stone. In the early days the quality of the stone was not very good and until today it is very hard to work with." Osuitok Ipeelee, in Susan Gustavison, Northern Rock: Contemporary Inuit stone sculpture, p. 63.

FROM PRIMITIVE TO MODERN TOOLS

Even more remarkable is the capacity to use basic hand tools to undertake sculpture in the round from the densest and hardest raw materials in the land. With almost nothing (hand-axes, mallets, knives, files and chisels) the sculptor manages to release the work, exploiting the properties of the material almost beyond the realm of the possible.

Direct and tactile contact with the material has persisted even with the more recent introduction of power tools, which artists quickly adapted to the roughing out and finishing stages. To protect themselves from the harmful mineral dust produced by grinders, artists usually do this very dirty physical work outside or in a makeshift shelter.

THE ULTIMATE TOUCH OF MAGIC

The last and most delicate final steps infuse a carving with life and soul, and require particular care. Many artists hand polish the stone with steel wool or emery paper. Some choose to blacken the sanded surfaces with ordinary products such as shoe polish to accentuate the curves and hollows. Others employ a clear wax used for marble to bring out the natural veins and colours in the stone.

Yet others take advantage of smooth or porous textures, incising designs or inlaying ivory, bone etc. Within the technical practices shared by all, there are as many approaches, nuances and sensitivities as there are artists, and numerous regional particularities.

Andy Mamgark, (1930-1997)
Arviat
Three Bears Playing, 1996
basalt
1998.486
7.9 × 29.2 × 19 cm

Pitseolak Niviaqsi, (born 1947)
Cape Dorset
Bird with Wings Spread, 1987
serpentinite
1998.585
24.5 × 22.5 × 9.3 cm

REGIONAL STYLES

Over the past 50 years the principal centres of production in the North have developed regional characteristics that account for the major trends in contemporary Inuit art. Regional styles develop when individual talent is drawn to the same community and then passes on that style, and also when the artistic life of a community is shaped by the same exterior influence, such as market pressure.

But the most determining factor remains the nature of the local carving material itself, whether stone is used, as in most places, or whalebone, more easily available in certain areas of the Central Arctic and Kitikmeot.

Uriash Puqiqnaq, (born 1946)
Gjoa Haven, Kitikmeot
Fishing Legend, 1996
pyroxene, muskox horn, sinew
2002.011
50 × 28.5 × 20 cm

Charlie Inukpuk, (born 1941)
Inukjuak, Nunavik
Woman Making Boot, 1980
steatite
1998.256
44.0 × 25.5 × 11.5 cm

Steatite or soapstone is plentiful in Nunavik (Northern Quebec), and is soft, lending itself to fine detail. It has occasioned a blossoming of figurative and naturalistic art, both strongly narrative and skilfully expressive.

For many Keewatin (Nunavut) sculptors, on the other hand, the hardness of the basalt rock has posed quite a challenge. Through skill and determination they have come up with pristine and expressive representations that verge on the abstract. Rugged, massive and crude, they blend the primitive and the indigenous into art that is essentially minimalist and modern: two powerful trends in current Inuit sculpture.

The skilful sculptors of southern Baffin Island and the flagship community of Cape Dorset carve whalebone, walrus ivory and varieties of stone such as serpentinite, or "Arctic jade" into captivating and often flamboyant works of art. Their stylized virtuosity is a response to the beauty and fragility of the material they work with, tapering it and piercing it almost to breaking point. The complexity and elegance of these incredibly light and delicate compositions that defy the laws of gravity and balance.

Lucy Tasseor Tutsweetok, (born 1934)
Arviat, Keewatin
Family, 1993
basalt
37.0 × 28.5 × 21.6 cm

Quvaroak Tunnillie, (1942-1993)
Cape Dorset, Baffin Island
Hunter Carrying Beluga, circa 1977
serpentinite
2002.013
36 × 38 × 16 cm

Artist unknown
Clyde River
Face, circa 1960
whalebone
17 × 22 × 6 cm

V

An autobiographical art

"WE CARVE THE ANIMALS because they are important to us as food. We carve Inuit figures because in that way we can show ourselves to the world as we were in the past and as we now are... There is nothing marvellous about it. It is there for everyone to see. It is just the truth." Paulosie Kasadluak, Inukjuak, 1976. Quoted by Ingo Hessel in *Inuit Art*, p. 37.

The concept of the primitive world as one powered by visible and invisible opposing forces that dominate every aspect of this mortal life provides fertile ground for the rich imaginary life of artists and a starting point for telling the story of their people. The creation myths, folk tales and fragments of history that make up the incredible Inuit odyssey, which has been passed down orally and which the artists want to convey, gives their art the quality of a collective memory.

Artist unknown
Baffin Island
*Mother and Child under
Shaman's Protection*, 1974
whalebone
2002.019
64.5 × 55 × 31 cm

THE VISIBLE WORLD

The superiority of contemporary Inuit artists in capturing meaning and emotion in sculpture lies in their perfect knowledge of the natural environment and the creatures that inhabit it, in their intimate knowledge of the anatomy of every animal and in the observation of animal habits and gestures upon which their hunting prowess once depended. Tales of the hunt and representations of arctic animal life thus predominate in the Inuit naturalist repertoire and in their imagery in general.

Under the carver's tools human life unfolds, practical, dramatic, tender and funny, scenes that charm with their narrative and verisimilitude, giving us a glimpse of the values and common attitudes of the past. The works of artists who prefer realism, widespread in Nunavik, can be a source of information for historians and ethnologists.

A family group, a mother with her child huddled in the hood of her *amautiq*, a woman busy sewing or cutting up meat with her *ulu*, a man boldly stalking his prey or pitted against his peers in games of skill and strength, all play an important role in the account of the ancient rites of daily life in this culture.

In contrast, the evocation of exploits, memories, happy and tragic anecdotes are also central concerns for those innovative artists who, in their private experiments, are expressing a new affirmation of the present and a desire to belong to the modern world.

Oomagajuk Tikivik, (born 1921)
Kimmirut
Hunter, 1975
serpentinite, walrus ivory, sinew
1998.195
23.2 × 29.2 × 13.4 cm

Josie Napartuk, (1901-1980)
Kuujjuaraapik
Bird Hunter, circa 1965
argilite, wood, ivory, string
1998.213
21 × 26 × 12.5 cm

Pitsiula Michael, (born 1965)
Kimmirut
*Hunter Hiding Behind
a Screen*, 1993
serpentinite, wood,
caribou antler, sealskin, sinew
1998.197
36 × 35 × 20.4 cm

Simeonie Elijassapik, (born 1948)
Inukjuak
Mother and Child, 1987
steatite
2002.010
39,5 × 10.8 × 40.5 cm

Pavinaq Petaulassie, (born 1961)
Cape Dorset
Caribou, 1996
serpentinite, caribou antler
1998.434
24.3 × 42 × 16 cm

THE INVISIBLE WORLD

The Inuit once knew how to live in harmony and equilibrium with nature, taming it and sowing it with the seeds of their nomadic existence. But they are powerless before invisible forces that they can neither understand nor control. Confronted with the occult and the supernatural and baffled by it, they consulted the *angatkuk* or *angakok,* the shaman. He or she alone held the key to the other world. Their magic, their gifts of mystification and powers as medium enabled them to intercede with the gods and spirits – good or evil – and to change into any animate or inanimate being in order to contact and appease them.

Some Inuit artists do not hesitate to "actualize" the beliefs that preceded their conversion to Christianity, using every medium and style. Recurrent themes draw on their animist spirituality, including shamanic rituals such as the drum dance, trances and the strange transformation of shamans into animals and vice versa. Dreams, fears and premonitions give rise to surrealist visions pregnant with symbolism.

The myths and legends have travelled orally through time and space, leaving in their wake dozens of versions and variants, each more captivating than the last. They are peopled by a fabulous bestiary and cast of superhuman characters, disembodied and grotesque beings who make up the great arctic mythology that the artist bequeaths to posterity.

Judas Ullulaq, (1937-1999)
Gjoa Haven
Transformation, 1994
Pyroxene, muskox horn, caribou antler, alabaster
10.2 × 45.9 × 11 cm

David Ruben Piqtoukun, (born 1950)
Paulatuk
Shaman from Walrus Territory, 1985
serpentinite, walrus ivory, caribou antler
1998.467
38.2 × 34.2 × 16.5 cm

Artist unknown
Clyde River
Spirit, circa 1980
whalebone, caribou antler, stone, metal
38.5 × 44.4 × 19.5 cm

Manasie Akpaliapik, (born 1955)
Arctic Bay
In Memory of a Drowning Accident, 1994
whalebone, caribou antler
2002.018
48.5 × 35 × 31.5 cm

Abraham Apakark Anghik, (born 1951)
Paulatuk
Transformations, 2000
Brazilian steatite
2002.025
49 × 36 × 15 cm

Osuitok Ipeelee, (born 1923)
Cape Dorset
Sedna, 1996
serpentinite
2002.021
28.5 × 42 × 18 cm

Qaunaq Palluq, (born 1936)
Clyde River
Sedna, 1996
whalebone
1998.475
22.6 × 48 × 19.2 cm

At once feared and venerated, goddess of the sea *Sedna* stands at the pinnacle of the Inuit pantheon, reigning over marine mammals and elements, and is one of the most ambivalent of Arctic mythical figures. Symbol of fertility and abundance, she is also known as *Taleelayu, Nuliajuk* or *Kavna,* "the one from below". She is generally described as a hybrid creature, half woman and half sea-mammal, like the mermaids of ancient western legends. By turns indulgent and tyrannical, she holds the destiny of human beings in her hands.

Toonoo Sharky, (born 1970)
Cape Dorset
Flying Spirit, 1999
stone, serpentinite, ivory
17.4 × 33.0 × 8.6 cm

Simon Tookoome, (born 1934)
Baker Lake
Reincarnation, 1990
basalt
1998.565
20.5 × 29.7 × 8.4 cm

VI

The Inuit artist

ONCE THE INUIT DISCOVERED that the strange figures they used to carve for pleasure had a certain monetary value "down south", they were driven by the outside world to pursue an artistic vocation together. Amazingly, art was the first step they took in embracing their new sedentary way of life and paradoxically, it also restored a tenuous link with their ancestors. It was the artists' task to sustain this heritage among their own people, and introduce it to the rest of the world.

STORY TELLERS AND GUARDIANS OF TRADITION

Inuit history was passed down orally, as it was among all isolated peoples of Africa, Australia and Oceania who were catapulted into the modern era. Artists have been foremost in preserving this rich cultural heritage over the past three generations, principally for their own people but also to signal its existence to southerners. Artists adopt in turn the role of story teller and guardian of the tradition. Their careers, now well established, have a scope that they could never have dreamed of.

Mattiusi Iyaituq, (born 1950)
Ivujivik
Shaman, 2000
serpentinite, bone, muskox hair
2002.017
59.5 × 25 × 16 cm

Jolly Aningmiuq, (1954-2000)
Cape Dorset
Figure Riding a Caribou, 1994
serpentinite, caribou antler
2002.004
66 × 66 × 40 cm

Qavaroak Tunnillie
(1928-1993)
Cape Dorset
Bird Legend
serpentinite
2002.003
73 × 38 × 17 cm

A RARE HISTORICAL PHENOMENON

The unrelenting involvement of the Canadian government in what would henceforth be known as the "artistic industry" of the North soon gave rise to little communities of carvers. So much so that almost all the adults in every single village threw themselves into it, both men and women. In 1951 this activity employed more than 70% of the active inhabitants of Salluit (Nunavik). A further example: in the mid-1960s among the 500-strong population of Baker Lake (Nunavut), more than 200 were involved in carving.[3]

While many Inuit tried their hand at art during this pioneer period, and especially carving, many later dropped it and in order to make ends meet took work instead in the new industries that were springing up in the Arctic: mining, infrastructure construction, administration and community services.

But for those who stayed in sculpture or who took to it over the next generations, the percentage of "good artists" relative to such a sparse population remains impressive, as George Swinton has noted.[4]

---

3. This significant data was recorded by Ingo Hessel in *Inuit Art*, p. 188.
4. George Swinton, *Sculpture of the Inuit*, p. 13.

Josiah Nuilaalik, (born 1928)
Baker Lake
Shaman from Caribou Territory, 1993
basalt, caribou antler, walrus ivory
1998.560
27 × 15 × 13.5 cm

Barnabus Arnasungaaq, (born 1924)
Baker Lake
Artist Carrying His Sculpture, 1990
basalt
1998.581
26.1 × 17.3 × 15.5 cm

George Arluk, (born 1949)
Arviat
Family, 1997
basalt
2002.006
54 × 40 × 12 cm

INDIVIDUAL ARTISTS

Aside from the ethnic interest and generic traits of the nascent "Eskimo art", significant individual talent emerged during the 1950s, revitalizing established forms and distinguishing themselves from repetitive and stagnant commercial over-production with a powerful stylistic personality and content that was evocative and timeless.

The sculptures that emerged from this exceptional artistic talent, some of them by unknown artists, elicited that state of wonder and heightened awareness that only true works of art can achieve.

The freshness of the artist's eye was seen in early days as uncorrupted by the western aesthetic canon, and attracted immediate attention.

Joseph Shuqslak, (born 1958)
Gjoa Haven
Smiling Man, 1999
pyroxene, bone
2002.092
24.5 × 18 × 11.5 cm

Jean-Marie Ivalutannar Oksokitok, (born 1944)
Repulse Bay
Mask, 1997
pyroxene
2002.235
18 × 18 × 8 cm

Ekidluak Komoartuk, (1923-1993)
Cape Dorset
Spirit, circa 1960
whalebone
23.5 × 33 × 14.5 cm

Artist unknown
Whale hunter, circa 1960
argilite, skin, wood,
rope, horn, baleen plate
1998.112
11.5 × 32 × 9 cm

Artist unknown
Standing figure, circa 1950
steatite
1998.036
15.5 × 5.5 × 4 cm

Johnny Kakutuk, (born 1946)
Akulivik
Hunter Carrying Seal, circa 1965
serpentinite
1998.190
27.5 × 15.4 × 16 cm

FROM ANONYMITY TO FAME

For a long time these works were shipped off to southern markets with no signatures except that of the Inuk delegated to collect the works from the villages. This has resulted in a serious problem of attribution, and conundrums for specialist research.

However, as Inuit artists gain in self-confidence, cooperatives organize themselves, and the public is increasingly ravenous for any information about the mysterious Arctic artists, names are becoming known, reputations are forged and fame takes shape.

The era of anonymity is long gone. After 50 years of continuous production, Inuit art has brought forth some true masters.

THE STATUS OF ARTIST

Professional Inuit artists, and there are currently several hundred, are economic forces in their communities and occupy the highest social position. Only the great hunters of the past, admired by all, have ever enjoyed such status.

Faithful to their traditional values of sharing and participation, artists take care of the needs of their immediate families, relations and neighbours. The direct or indirect financial spin-offs of their success benefit the whole community. In a region that is socially and economically deprived, cooperatives provide stable jobs, and the lucrative "artistic industry" has become a focus of national pride.

AMBASSADORS AND GLOBETROTTERS

Artists of today no longer live a completely self-sufficient lifestyle. While art was seen as an honourable way for the elderly to earn a living, for a number of talented youth now see it as their vocation. The careers of some have taken an enviable international direction, with their work in high demand for exhibitions in the US, Europe, Asia and elsewhere. As artists they are asked to participate in symposia and conferences worldwide, and become representatives and ambassadors for their people. Travel also connects these sensitive artists with other cultures and influences, and advances in telecommunications (radio, television, internet, etc) have added new models, icons, modes of expression, techniques, concerns and themes to their daily horizon.

Nuveeya Ipellie, (born 1920)
Iqaluit
Muskox, 1992
serpentinite, caribou antler
2000.258
20.5 × 30.5 × 10 cm

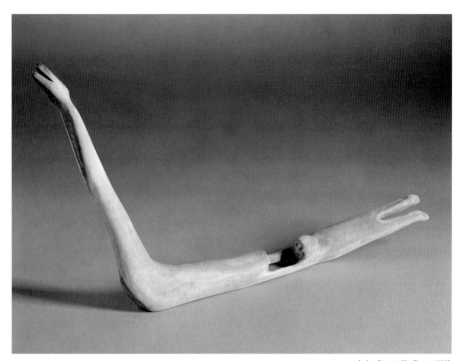

Luke Anowtalik, (born 1932)
Arviat
The Legend of Lummaq, 1992
caribou antler
1998.470
23.5 × 40.3 × 5.5 cm

Kaka Ashoona, (1928-1996)
Cape Dorset
Head of a Woman, 1990
serpentinite
2002.027
29 × 21.5 × 32 cm

Manasie Akpaliapik, (born 1955)
Arctic Bay
Woman from Alaska, 1996
whalebone, caribou antler, stone
2002.002
20.4 × 84 × 43 cm

Peter Morgan, (born 1951)
Kangiqsualujjuaq
Caribou Spirit
caribou antler, black ink, horn, steatite
2002.008
100 × 100 × 60 cm

CONCLUSION

The universal scope of Inuit art

Although today's Inuit would never consider returning to the dangerous and difficult life led by their ancestors in their igloos, their art rears up as if to exorcise their fear of acculturation and assimilation. Art has become one of the last bastions against insidious forgetfulness, a defensive reflex against the irretrievable loss of their aboriginal identity.

Art is not a permanent fixture. The language of artists evolves, transcending trends, time, and space. Over the past 50 years Inuit sensibility has integrated many materials in addition to stone and bone, and has adopted techniques less traditional than sculpture. Printing (lithography, serigraphy, etching), drawing, and textile arts are examples. Pottery and even jewellery are also emerging visual arts.

Cutting-edge technologies are involved in promoting and exporting Inuit culture on a large scale. Digital art, video and cinema are increasingly used as communication techniques. *Atanaarjuat,* or the *Legend of the Fast Runner,* the feature film by Zacharias Kunuk that won the Camera d'Or at the Cannes International Film Festival in 2001, is a good illustration of this new openness to the world, and the world's recognition of Inuit culture.

In spite of a perspective that is surreptitiously becoming more and more westernized, and an aesthetic that is gradually permitting more blending and hybridity, Inuit art of the twenty-first century will always remain profoundly Inuit, as its creators are, above all, northern natives who bear the heavy responsibility of cultural, and not just physical, survival.

The desire to tell their story in their own terms or in their own language overrides all kinds of other motivations. Nothing and no-one can appropriate their creative memory or dilute their originality. The shadow of their forms, modes of expression and themes has lengthened, but the scope of their message remains universal.

"I would go back to the law of the Inuit, the law of nature. I would live like that while checking e-mail in the morning, calling halfway around the world to do business [...]. It is possible to do both in this day. " Zacharias Kunuk, filmmaker. *New York Times,* March 30, 2002.

TIMELINE

5000 – 1000 BCE

- First great migration from Siberia to Alaska across the Bering Strait. Beginnings of sporadic human presence in the Canadian Arctic.

Circa 1000 BCE – circa 1000 CE

- The Dorset Culture. The Dorsets left behind small figurative sculptures of stone and ivory with magical or religious significance, closely linked to shamanic rituals.

Circa 1000 CE – 1700-1800

- Thule Culture. This last migration signalled the decline of the Dorset culture. Thule people were pragmatic hunters, mostly of whales and other marine mammals, and with their material progress (more effective hunting and survival techniques) they overran their predecessors. They also developed a more elegant and decorative art by incising stylized patterns on their implements, imbuing them with occult powers.

1576

- Earliest European expeditions to the Arctic in search of the Northwest Passage and the spices of China. Contacts with Inuit were very rare.

1771

- Arrival of the Moravian Brothers, a Protestant denomination from Germany, who established the first mission at Nain, in Labrador. For evangelistic purposes they developed a Roman orthography for Inuktitut, which up to that time had only been oral. This was the first Inuit introduction to writing, and marks the beginning of the Historic Period.

Circa 1800 – circa 1900

- The demand for whale oil increased with industrialization, as it was used for running machinery and as a lighting fuel. Often trapped for months in the ice, the whalers had prolonged contact with Inuit, with whom they exchanged technical skills and implements.

1948

- James Houston's travels in the North. His discovery of Inuit art and the start of a momentum to develop it.

1949-1955

- First tangible commercialization campaign by the Montreal-based Canadian Guild of Crafts and the Canadian government to acquaint all Canadians with Inuit art.

1959-1967

- Creation of local cooperatives, under the auspices of the Quebec and Canadian governments and La Fédération des Caisses Populaires Desjardins, for developing and marketing Inuit art. The cooperatives assured that the Inuit were justly remunerated for their creations.

1967

- The Montreal World's Fair (Expo '67) : Inuit art is recognized in an exhibition of sculptures and engravings at the Canadian Pavillion, making Inuit art renown the world over.

1971

- Publicaton of the first exhaustive study of Inuit art, *Sculpture of the Inuit* by Professor George Swinton.

1971-1973

- Following the international demand created by Expo '67, the exhibition *Masterworks of the Canadian Arctic* tours the world (Moscow, Leningrad, Paris, London, Philadelphia).

1989

- World tour of exhibition *Masters of the Arctic* opens at the United Nations headquarters in New York, then in South America and Japan.

1998

- Musée d'art INUIT Brousseau is founded in Quebec City, the first museum south of the Arctic dedicated exclusively to Inuit art.

1999

- Nunavut, the third Canadian territory, is created out of the former Northwest Territories. Its population is 85% Inuit, and the new government takes over responsibility for Inuit health, education and justice.

2002

- The Lyons Natural History Museum, in collaboration with the Musée d'art INUIT Brousseau, opens an important exhibition of Inuit art (750 m2./7500 sq.ft.) in December that will tour Europe for nearly 5 years.

Manasie Akpaliapik, (born 1955)
Arctic Bay
Maternity, 2001
whalebone
117 x 42 x 45 cm

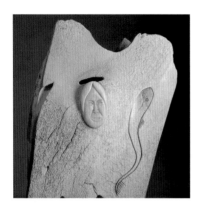

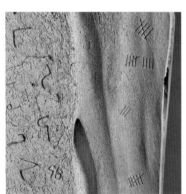

BIBLIOGRAPHY OF INUIT ART

Georges-Hébert GERMAIN, *Les Peuples du froid.*
ed. MORRISSON, David. Éditions
Libre Expression, Montreal/
Museum of Civilisations, Hull, 1995.

Susan GUSTAVSON, et al. *Northern Rock:
Contemporary Inuit Stone Sculpture.*
McMichael Canadian Art Collection,
Kleinburg, 1999.

Ingo HESSEL. *Inuit Art: An Introduction.* British
Museum, London, 1998.

Jean MALAURIE, ed. *L'Art du grand Nord.*
Citadelles et Mazenod, Paris, 2001.

Harold SEIDELMAN & James TURNER. *The Inuit
Imagination: Arctic Myth and Culture.*
Douglas & McInytre Ltd., Vancouver and
Toronto, 1993.

George SWINTON. *Sculpture of the Inuit*, 3d
Edition, rev. and updated. McClelland &
Stewart Inc./The Canadian Publishers,
Toronto, 1999 [1971].

ISBN 2-9807610-1-X
Legal deposit - Bibliothèque nationale du Québec, 2002
Legal deposit - National Library of Canada, 2002

TABLE OF CONTENTS

Index of Artists

Luke **Airut**, Igloolik, Baffin Island

Manasie **Akpaliapik**, Arctic Bay, Baffin Island

Abraham **Anghik**, Paulatuk, Kitikmeot

Jolly **Aningmiuq**, *Cape Dorset*, Baffin Island

Luke **Anowtalik**, *Arviat*, Keewatin

George **Arluk**, *Arviat*, Keewatin

Barnabus **Arnasungaaq**, *Baker Lake*, Keewatin

Kaka **Ashoona**, Cape Dorset, Baffin Island

Simionie **Elijassapik**, *Inukjuak*, Nunavik

Simon **Hiqiniq**, *Gjoa Haven*, Kitikmeot

Charlie **Inukpuk**, *Inukjuak*, Nunavik

Osiutok **Ipeelee**, *Cape Dorset*, Baffin Island

Nuveeya **Ipellie**, *Iqaluit*, Baffin Island

Jaco **Ishulutaq**, *Pangnirtung*, Baffin Island

John **Ivalutannar**, *Repulse Bay*, Keewatin

Mattiusi **Iyaituk**, *Ivujivik*, Nunavik

Pootoogook **Jaw**, *Cape Dorset*, Baffin Island

Johnny **Kakutuk**, *Akulivik*, Nunavik

Towkie **Karpik**, *Pangnirtung*, Baffin Island

Paulosie **Kasudluak**, *Inukjuak*, Nunavik

John **Kavik**, Rankin Inlet, Keewatin

Ross **Kayotak**, *Igloolik*, Baffin Island

Kiakshuk, Cape Dorset, Baffin Island

Shorty **Killiktee**, *Kimmirut*, Baffin Island

Ekidluak **Komoartuk**, *Cape Dorset*, Baffin Island

Joanassie **Korgak**, *Iqaluit*, Baffin Island

Elijah **Kuppak**, *Arctic Bay*, Baffin Island

Andy **Mamgark**, *Arviat*, Keewatin

Pitsiula **Michael**, *Kimmirut*, Baffin Island

Peter **Morgan**, Kangiqsualujjuaq, Nunavik

Josie **Napartuk**, *Kuujjuaraapik*, Nunavik

Samson **Nastapoka**, *Inukjuak*, Nunavik

(Pierre) **Nauya**, *Rankin Inlet*, Keewatin

Pitseolak **Niviaqsi**, *Cape Dorset*, Baffin Island

Josiah **Nuilaalik**, *Baker Lake*, Keewatin

Isa **Oomayoualook**, *Inukjuak*, Nunavik

Qaunaq **Palluq**, *Clyde River*, Baffin Island

Aoudla **Pee**, Cape Dorset, Baffin Island

Pavinaq **Petaulassie**, *Cape Dorset*, Baffin Island

David Ruben **Piqtoukun**, Paulatuk, Kitikmeot

Uriash Puqiqnaq, *Gjoa Haven*, Kitikmeot

Isapik **Qanguq**, *Pond Inlet*, Baffin Island

Pauta **Saila**, Cape Dorset, Baffin Island

Qiatsuq **Shaa**, Cape Dorset, Baffin Island

Toonoo **Sharky**, *Cape Dorset*, Baffin Island

Joseph **Shuqslak**, *Gjoa Haven*, Kitikmeot

Joanassie **Smith**, *Puvirnituq*, Nunavik

Joe **Talirunili**, *Puvirnituq*, Nunavik

Oomagajuk **Tikivik**, *Kimmirut*, Baffin Island

Simon **Tookoome**, *Baker Lake*, Keewatin

Qavaroak **Tunnillie**, *Cape Dorset*, Baffin Island

Lucy Tasseor **Tutsweetok**, *Arviat*, Keewatin

Judas **Ullulaq**, *Gjoa Haven*, Kitikmeot

CARTOGRAPHY:
Frida Franco, *graphic artist.*

CANADIAN ARCTIC ART CENTRES

...arbour

▲ Resolute

▲ Arctic Bay

Groenland

Région de
l'ÎLE DE BAFFIN
BAFFIN ISLAND

▲ Clyde River

cercle polaire — Polar circle

Région du
KITIKMEOT

...ktuk

▲ Taloyoak   ▲ Igloolik

▲ Broughton Island

▲ Gjoa Haven

▲ Pelly Bay

▲ Pangnirtung

Repulse Bay ▲

Région du
KIVALLIQ
(KEEWATIN)

▲ Iqaluit

▲ Cape Dorset

Baker Lake ▲

▲ Kimmirut

Rankin Inlet ▲   ▲ Chesterfield
Inlet

Ivujivik ▲   Salluit ▲

▲ Killiniq

Whale Cove ▲

Akulivik ▲

Kangiqsujuaq ▲

▲ Arviat

Région du
NUNAVIK

▲ Kangiqsualujjuaq

Kuujjuaq ▲

▲ Nain

Puvirnituq ▲

ligne des arbres — tree line

Baie d'Hudson

Inukjuak ▲

● Churchill

▲ Rigolet

Sanikiluaq ▲

Labrador

Kuujjuaraapik ▲

Québec

⬛ NUNAVUT

Québec ●

ECHELLE — SCALE

Montréal — Québec

Montréal ●

300 Km
180 miles

New York ↓

CREDITS

Principal source:	Raymond Brousseau, Founding Director and Curator of the Musée d'art INUIT Brousseau
Research and Text:	Nicole Allard, jbenoigt@globetrotter.net
Coordination:	Diane Bradette
Editing:	Annie Hudon
Artistic supervision:	Lyse Brousseau
Additional sources:	Marie-Hélène Brais, Louise Pépin, Françoise Villeneuve-Hocq, Hélène Dussault
Photographs and image processing:	Paul Dionne, pdionne@pdionne-photo.qc.ca
Graphics:	Norman Dupuis Inc., normandupuis@sympatico.ca
Translation:	Louisa Blair, lblair@total.net
Published by:	**Musée d'art INUIT Brousseau** 39, rue Saint-Louis, Vieux-Québec (Québec) Canada G1R 3Z2 418 694 1828

artinuit@globetrotter.net
www.inuitart.ca

ACKNOWLEDGEMENTS

We would like to express our gratitude to Mrs. Diane Lemieux, Minister of Culture and Communications of the Government of Quebec, for her moral and financial support and to Mrs Agnès Maltais deputy of Taschereau and Minister for Employment.

We would also like to thank the museum staff for their involvement with the public and their essential contribution to the dissemination of Inuit art.